Contents

Why do you get thirsty? 4

Why do you need to drink? 6

Do drinks have water in them? 8

Does food have water in it? 10

Making orange juice! 12

When do you need to drink most? 14

How do you lose the most water? . . . 16

What happens if you do not
drink enough? 18

Keep drinking! 20

How much do you need to drink? 22

Glossary 23

Index 24

Note to parents and teachers 24

Why do you get thirsty?

You feel thirsty when your body needs more water.

Your mouth goes dry.

When you drink you give your body
the water it needs.

Why do you need to drink?

Your body loses water every day.

Pee, **sweat** and tears are mostly water.

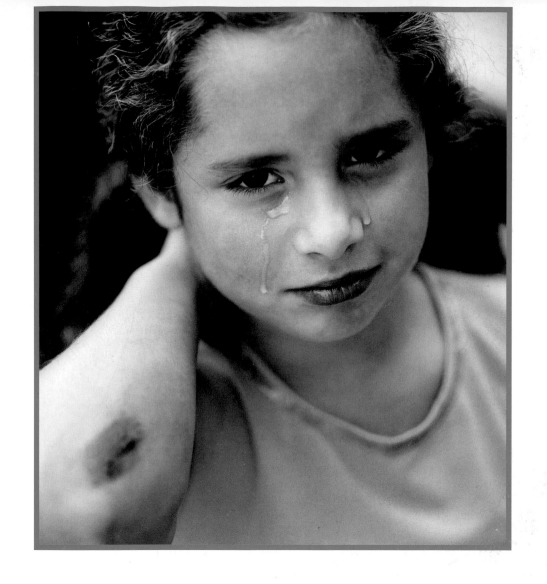

Blood and **mucus** are mostly water.

When you drink you put back the water you lose.

Do drinks have water in them?

All drinks have water in them.

Most drinks are water mixed with other things.

Most fizzy drinks also have sugar in them.

Water is the best drink to have!

Does food have water in it?

All food has some water in it.

Fruit and vegetables have the most.

Oranges are full of juice.

Do you know how to make orange juice?

Making orange juice!

1. Ask an adult to cut four large oranges in half.

2. Using a juicer, squeeze each half.

3. Pour the orange juice into a glass.

4. Enjoy drinking your fresh orange juice!

When do you need to drink most?

You need to drink most when you are hot.

You **sweat** more when you are hot.

When you sweat, you lose
more water.

How do you lose the most water?

You lose most water when you pee.

You should pee several times a day.

Pee is one way your body gets rid of waste.

Do not forget to wash your hands afterwards!

What happens if you do not drink enough?

If you do not drink enough water, you will get **dehydrated**.

If you get dehydrated, you might get a headache.

Drinking some water might help.

Keep drinking!

Drink two glasses of water.

Drink two more glasses of water an hour later. What happens?

You should need to go to
the toilet.

But you should also feel more
lively and healthy.

How much do you need to drink?

You should drink four glasses a day.

Drink more if you are very active.

Glossary

 **dehydrated** not having enough water

 **mucus** kind of liquid made inside your body. Snot is a kind of mucus.

 **sweat** salty water made by your body. Sweat comes out through your skin.

Index

drinking water 5, 7, 9, 18, 19, 20, 21, 22

food 10

losing water 6, 7, 15, 16

orange juice 11, 12, 13

pee 6, 16, 17

sweat 6, 14, 15

Note to parents and teachers

Reading non-fiction texts for information is an important part of a child's literacy development. Readers can be encouraged to ask simple questions and then use the text to find the answers. Most chapters in this book begin with a question. Read the questions together. Look at the pictures. Talk about what the answer might be. Then read the text to find out if your predictions were correct. To develop readers' enquiry skills, encourage them to think of other questions they might ask about the topic. Discuss where you could find the answers. Assist children in using the contents page, picture glossary and index to practise research skills and new vocabulary.

Why do we need to drink water?

Angela Royston

www.raintreepublishers.co.uk
Visit our website to find out more information about **Raintree** books.

To order:
☎ Phone 44 (0) 1865 888112
🖹 Send a fax to 44 (0) 1865 314091
💻 Visit the Raintree Bookshop at **www.raintreepublishers.co.uk** to browse our catalogue and order online.

First published in Great Britain by Raintree,
Halley Court, Jordan Hill, Oxford OX2 8EJ,
part of Harcourt Education.
Raintree is a registered trademark of Harcourt
Education Ltd.

© Harcourt Education Ltd 2006
First published in paperback in 2007
The moral right of the proprietor has
been asserted.

Editorial: Jilly Attwood
Design: Jo Hinton-Malivoire, bigtop
Picture Research: Ruth Blair, Ginny Stroud-Lewis
Production: Severine Ribierre
Originated by Modern Age
Printed and bound in China by South China
Printing Company

10 digit ISBN 1 4062 0049 2 (hardback)
13 digit ISBN 978 1 4062 0049 2 (hardback)
10 09 08 07 06
10 9 8 7 6 5 4 3 2 1
10 digit ISBN 1 406 20054 9 (paperback)
13 digit ISBN 978 1 406 20054 6 (paperback)
11 10 09 08 07
10 9 8 7 6 5 4 3 2 1

British Library Cataloguing in Publication Data
Royston, Angela
Why do we need to drink water?. - (Stay
healthy!)
613.2'87

A full catalogue record for this book is available
from the British Library.

Acknowledgements
The publishers would like to thank the following
for permission to reproduce photographs:
Corbis pp.4, 20(Norbert Schaefer); p.5(Richard T.
Nowitz) p.14(Gabe Palmer); Getty Images pp.6,
18(Stone), pp.7, 23b(Digital Vision), p.15, p.19,
23a, 23c(Photodisc); Harcourt Education pp.8, 9,
12(Gareth Boden), pp.11, 13, 16, 17, 21, 22
(Tudor Photography); Science Photo Library p.10.

Cover photograph of boy with water spout
reproduced with permission of Corbis. Back cover
images reproduced with permission of Harcourt
Education/ Gareth Boden and Tudor Photography.

Every effort has been made to contact copyright
holders of any material reproduced in this book.
Any omissions will be rectified in subsequent
printings if notice is given to the publishers.

Our thanks to Dr Sarah Schenker, Dietitian, for
her help in the preparation of this book.

Some words are shown in bo
find them in the picture gloss